0 5 MAY 2000

D1098337

Missing Statue

Gladstone Day
The man who wrote
The Science of Running

Alex Lane
Illustrated by Jon Stuart

9030 00000 0552 5

How to use this book ...

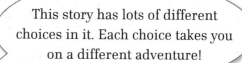

This story has lots of different choices in it. Each choice takes you on a different adventure!

There are instructions at the bottom of the pages for you to follow:

Decision boxes ... these are choices for you to make. There will be a question to help you. **?**

Move on boxes ... these are instructions for you to follow. **>**

Journey end boxes ... this means that you have come to an end. But don't worry, you can always start reading again and choose a different route! **●**

GREENVILLE NEWS

Scientist Statue Stolen!

The statue of the famous scientist Gladstone Day has gone missing. The statue, normally found in Green Bank Park, has not been seen since Saturday. Inspector Textor of the Greenville City Police Department said that they have carried out a full search of the area but cannot find it anywhere.

As a part-time sculptor, Mr Day made the statue of himself as a self-portrait just before he died. Three years ago, Mr Day's daughter, Dani, gave the statue to Green Bank Park so that everyone in the city could see it. The police are still trying to trace her to let her know that it has gone missing.

Max, Cat, Ant and Tiger are in the park. They are standing next to the plinth, where the statue of Gladstone Day should have been.

"Why would anyone want to steal a statue?" says Cat.

"Search me," shrugs Max.

"I don't know what all the fuss is about," says Tiger. "It's only a bit of stone."

Ant is very upset. Gladstone Day is one of his all time favourite heroes.

"Just a bit of stone!" he fumes. "It was made by Gladstone himself!"

"Who was he anyway?" asks Cat.

"Only the best scientist ever," says Ant. "He invented loads of cool micro stuff."

"Like what?" scoffs Tiger.

"Like the *Gladstone What-chip*," says Ant.

"The thing you stick in your ear?" says Max. "That answers any question you think of?"

"Yes," said Ant. "It links directly to the Internet and gives you lots of answers in seconds."

"Oh, *them*," says Cat. "They're cool. But it still doesn't explain why anyone would want to steal his statue."

Max scratches his head. "Maybe we should do some investigating ourselves."

"Really?" says Ant, hopefully.

"Sure," says Max. "Let's split up into pairs and see what we can find out."

Gladstone Day
The man who wrote
The Science of Running

Decision: Who do you want to go with?

To go with Max and Tiger, turn to page 6.
To go with Cat and Ant, turn to page 8.

Max and Tiger decide to search the area for clues. Max goes one way, Tiger the other.

It has been raining and the ground is soft.

"See anything?" calls out Max, after a few minutes.

"Nothing yet," says Tiger. Then, "Hang on ..."

"What is it?"

"I've found some tracks."

Gladstone Day
The man who wrote
The Science of Running

Max rushes over. Tiger crouches down.

"Look!" he says.

"Tyre tracks," whispers Max. "I didn't think that cars were allowed in the park."

"They're not," says Tiger. "But these weren't made by a car. These were made by a truck."

"The sort of truck that might be able to carry a heavy statue away?"

"Exactly!" says Tiger.

"I think we should follow them," says Max. "What do you think?"

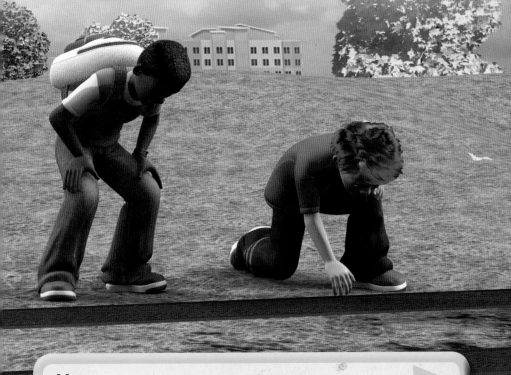

Move on
Follow the tyre tracks. Turn to page 10.

Cat and Ant look at the plinth where the statue once stood.

"What do you think, Ant?" says Cat.

"The statue is large and heavy. I don't know how they got it off the plinth."

"Maybe we should take a closer look," suggests Cat.

Ant understands right away. They turn the dials on their watches. They push the X and ...

Micro-size, Cat and Ant get a closer look at the base of the statue.

"Interesting," says Ant, running his hand across the stone. "It's completely smooth."

"Could it have been done with some sort of laser cutting machine?" asks Cat.

"Yes," says Ant. "Or *machines*."

"Are you thinking what I am thinking?" asks Cat.

"X-bots!" they both say together.

Gladstone Day
The man who wrote
The Science of Running

Move on
Find out if there are X-bots about. Turn to page 12.

"Let's go!" says Tiger. "They must lead us to the statue!"

Max and Tiger follow the tracks across the park and out of the gates. There, the tracks turn left.

"It's a good job it rained so hard," says Max. "All the mud has stuck to the tyres."

Max and Tiger keep going. They turn right, then another left.

"How much further?" says Tiger, after they have been going for some time.

"Look!" says Max, pointing up the street.

Up ahead is a sign. It says *RASCAL'S TRUCK HIRE*. The tracks lead right up to a big entrance.

"What now?" says Tiger.

Move on
Find out what they decide to do. Turn to page 14.

Ant wants to go back to their old micro-den, in the tree stump. He knows there are some magnets there. Magnets can be used to help stop X-bots and he wants to be ready, just in case.

When they get back to the micro-den, they find it in a complete mess.

"Not even Tiger is this messy!" says Ant. "Someone has been in here."

"Or *something*," says Cat with a shiver.

They hear a scuffling noise. It is coming from behind the upturned table.

"What's that?" says Cat.

But before Ant can answer, a scary black X-bot crashes out. It bleeps and hisses and snaps its jaws.

The children freeze.

"I think we should get out of here," squeaks Cat.

"Wait!" says Ant. "I've got an idea."

Decision: What should Cat and Ant do?

Find out about Ant's idea. Turn to page 16.
Get out of the room now! Turn to page 21.

Max and Tiger push open the door to the shop.
The bell above the door tinkles. There is a tall, thin
man with a beard behind the counter. A big book is
open in front of him. The man looks up when the two
children come in.

"Yeah?" says the man.

"Can you tell me," asks Max, politely. "Did you hire
any vans out on Saturday?"

The man narrows his eyes.

"We're closed on Saturdays," he says. "No vans were hired from here." He snaps the book in front of him shut.

"But ..." says Tiger.

"OK, thank you," says Max, butting in.

Max and Tiger go back outside.

"I don't think he was telling the truth," says Tiger.

"No, he wasn't," says Max, pointing to a sign in the window.

"So what do we do now?" says Tiger.

Rascal's Van Hire

opening times

Monday: 9am – 5pm

Tuesday: 9am – 5pm

Wednesday: closed

Thursday: 9am – 5pm

Friday: 9am – 5pm

Saturday: 10am – 4pm

Sunday: closed

Move on

Find out what happens next. Turn to page 18.

The X-bot moves towards Cat and Ant, snapping its jaws angrily.

"What are we going to do, Ant?" says Cat, scared.

Ant spots the magnet near the stairs.

"When I say, run for the stairs."

The X-bot takes another step towards them.

"Ant," wails Cat.

"NOW!" he yells.

Cat and Ant run towards the stairs. The X-bot runs after them. All of a sudden Ant turns sharp right.

"Ant!" cries Cat.

"Keep going!" Ant shouts back.

Cat disappears down the stairs.

Thinking that it has him cornered, the X-bot chases after Ant. But Ant makes a big jump and leaps over the magnet.

The X-bot follows, but as it scrambles over the magnet, it stops. Its eyes start to go funny, it sticks to the magnet and starts to quiver and fizz.

Ant runs down the stairs after Cat.

X3
N.A.S.T.I.

Move on
Find out what happens next. Turn to page 24.

Max and Tiger turn the dials on their watches. They push the X and ...

There is a gap under the door, wide enough for micro-Max and Tiger to crawl under.

The tall man is nowhere to be seen.

"What now?" asks Tiger.

"Let's get up on to the counter for a closer look round," says Max.

Max takes off his backpack. In it there is some string. Tiger finds a paperclip on the floor. They bend it and tie it to the string. Max throws it up and it hooks on to the side of the counter. One at a time, Max and Tiger climb up.

"Let's take a look at that book," says Max. "See if there are any clues."

They run across to the big book that is lying on the counter. Together they heave it open and turn the pages.

"Nothing," says Tiger.

All of a sudden the tall man with the beard comes back.

"Quick ..." says Max.

Decision: What should Max and Tiger do?

Run away. Turn to page 20.
Stay and hide. Turn to page 22.

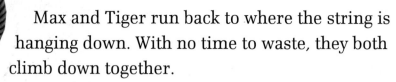

Max and Tiger run back to where the string is hanging down. With no time to waste, they both climb down together.

Halfway down, the string snaps. Max and Tiger tumble towards the ground.

Luckily, they fall into a waste paper bin and onto a thick bed of paper.

Unluckily, they can't grow back to normal size in the bin. They are stuck.

Journey end
With no way out, Max and Tiger have to wait until the bin is emptied. Your journey ends here! Return to page 5 and start again.

The X-bot takes a step towards Cat and Ant. It gives a metallic hiss.

"No, Ant! This is no time for clever ideas," says Cat, firmly. "Let's go NOW!"

Ant sees there's no arguing. "OK."

They begin to back slowly towards the stairs, one step at a time. The X-bot follows them, snapping and hissing.

When they are near the top step, Cat shouts, "RUN!"

It's a good job Cat and Ant are fast runners. They speed down two flights of stairs in no time. The X-bot clatters down the stairs behind them. But its legs get crossed and it falls over. The X-bot tumbles past them and lands in a heap on the floor. Ant gives it a kick. It does not move.

Move on
Find out what happens next. Turn to page 24.

Max and Tiger crouch down by the side of the book.

"Those two children looked familiar," says the tall man out loud.

Another man comes out of the back room. He is shorter but also has a beard.

"All children look the same to me," he says.

"We wouldn't have had to come back at all if you hadn't forgotten to put the keys back."

"I thought you were in charge of the keys!" whines the shorter man.

"No, that was your job. Don't worry. Here they are," says the tall man, putting a set of keys on the counter. "Now when Mr Rascal comes back from his holiday, he'll never know someone borrowed his truck to steal the statue."

"It was them!" whispers Tiger. "But why?"

"And where is the statue now?" says Max.

The tall man pulls off his beard. "This thing is itchy."

"A fake!" says Tiger.

"Plug and Socket!" says Max.

Move on
Find out what happens next. Turn to page 26.

Cat and Ant reach the bottom of the steps.

"If there are X-bots involved, we have to warn Max and Tiger," says Cat, gasping for breath.

"Let's take the buggy," says Ant.

They run across to the micro-buggy which is parked near the entrance.

"Great, I'll drive," says Cat, jumping into the driver's seat.

"Err, your watch is the only one that can track Max and Tiger," Ant points out. "You can't look at your watch *and* drive."

Cat sighs, but she knows Ant is right. So she shuffles across to the passenger seat and straps herself in.

Ant starts the micro-buggy.

"Here we go," says Ant excitedly. He puts it into reverse by accident and crashes into the tree stump. "Oops!" Ant blushes then slams the buggy forwards.

Soon, they are zooming out across the park.

Cat flips up her watch. She spots a blue and a red dot on the screen.

"I've got a position on Max and Tiger," she calls out to Ant.

Move on
Follow Cat and Ant in the micro-buggy.
Turn to page 28.

"We better get back," says Socket. "Otherwise the boss will be wondering where we are."

"I'll just put this book back," says Plug.

"Oh, no!" whispers Tiger, "we'll get caught."

"No we won't!" says Max. "Follow me."

Max and Tiger creep out from behind the book. They run across to the fake beard and hide in the thick hair.

"Socket was right," says Tiger. "It is itchy."

"Sssssshhh," hushes Max.

"Don't forget your beard," says Plug. "I'm quite attached to mine!"

Plug hands Socket the fake beard. Socket reluctantly stuffs the beard in his pocket ... along with Max and Tiger!

Plug and Socket leave *RASCAL'S TRUCK HIRE* by the back entrance.

BOOKINGS

Move on
Follow Plug and Socket. Turn to page 30.

"We need to head out of the park," says Cat. "Towards the city."

Ant drives the micro-buggy close to the bushes. When he is by the park gates, he turns left.

Cat checks her watch again. "They seem to be moving now. I hope we can catch them!"

"Don't worry," says Ant, "I've made a few modifications to the buggy."

"Modifi ... *what*?" says Cat.

"I've put another battery on. It means we can go faster."

Ant taps a button and ... *VROOM!* They are suddenly travelling at twice the speed.

The city is very busy. Luckily, most people are too busy looking in shop windows to notice two micro-children in a buggy whizzing by. But Ant still has to be careful steering round them.

"Watch out!" screams Cat, as Ant swerves around a pushchair. She is petrified, so she tries to concentrate on tracking Max and Tiger rather than on Ant's driving. "Right. Go right," she says.

Ant yanks the steering wheel round to the right and they fly off the kerb into the road.

Agghhhhhh!

Move on
Find out if Cat and Ant get across the road safely.
Turn to page 31.

Plug and Socket walk down the road. They head towards the NICE building - and their NASTI hideout underneath it.

"I'm hungry," says Plug. "Can we stop for ice cream?"

"We have to get back. The boss will be mad otherwise," says Socket.

"The boss is always mad," reasons Plug.

Decision: What should Plug and Socket do?

Carry on to NASTI. Move on to page 32.
Stop for ice cream. Turn to page 35.

The traffic begins to slow.

"Why are the cars slowing down?" asks Cat.

"Must be the traffic lights," replies Ant.

Ant steers easily between the car wheels. They get to the other side of the road and bump up on to the pavement.

"The signal is getting stronger," says Cat. "Straight on."

But then they see where they are heading ... straight for the NICE building.

"Oh, no!" gulps Ant.

"If they are going to NICE, it can only mean one thing ..." says Cat.

"NASTI," says Ant. "Dr X must be behind this. That means Max and Tiger might be in trouble."

Move on
Find out what happens next. Turn to page 33.

"No!" says Socket. "No ice cream."

When Plug and Socket get to the NICE building. They take the lift down to Floor X. They come out in a large room. There are computer screens everywhere and some very flashy machines and laboratory equipment. This is NASTI!

They take their coats off and hang them on a hook next to some white lab coats.

Still in Socket's pocket, Max and Tiger are hung up, too. They peek out.

Move on
Find out what happens next. Turn to page 38.

"We have to get in there," says Cat.

Ant drives the micro-buggy towards the front entrance of the NICE building. The doors to the large office block slide open. He steers past the reception desk where a woman is busy at a computer. She does not notice the small car on the floor.

"They are somewhere below," says Cat.

"NASTI is beneath this building," says Ant. "That means we have to go down."

"How?"

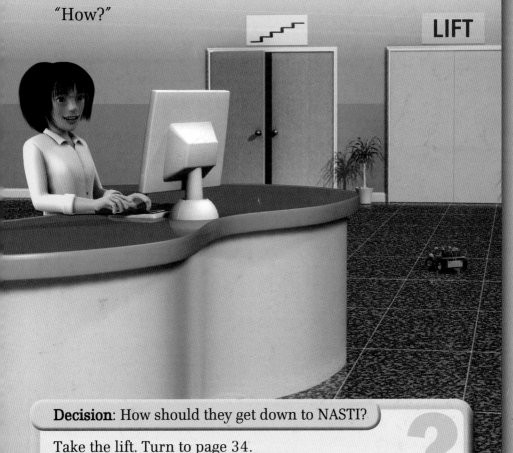

Decision: How should they get down to NASTI?

Take the lift. Turn to page 34.
Take the stairs. Turn to page 36.

Ant drives the micro-buggy up to the doors of the lift. They are too small to reach the button.

"We'll have to wait until someone comes," says Cat.

They don't have to wait long. *BING!* The lift doors open and a group of chattering people come out. Ant puts his foot down and drives into the lift. When the doors close it is safe for them to grow back to normal.

Cat looks at the row of buttons and pushes the bottom one. The lift begins to go down but after a few seconds there is a loud *CLUNK*. The lift stops. The doors do not open.

Journey end

Oh no! Cat and Ant are stuck in the lift. They will have to wait until the engineer is called. Your journey ends here!

Plug and Socket go into the ice-cream shop. They stare at the rows of ice cream lined up in tubs before them.

"Chocolate or vanilla?" says Plug, jumping up and down excitedly. "I know, I'll have both."

"Make that two of both," says Socket, to the woman behind the counter. "With sprinkles."

Journey end
Plug and Socket eat their ice creams. Then they order more. And more ... Max and Tiger are stuck. Your journey ends here!

"I know we'll take the lift," says Ant.

"I don't like lifts," says Cat. "What if we get stuck?"

"We'll have to go down the stairs then."

Ant steers the micro-buggy across to a door that is propped open. There is no way that they can get down the steps in the micro-buggy. So, out of sight, they grow back to normal size. Then they go down the stairs to the basement. Cat carries the micro-buggy.

"Max and Tiger aren't here," says Cat. "My watch says that they are further down."

They go down some more steps until they get to a big door that says: PRIVATE. NO ENTRY!

Ant pushes the door open. They walk to the end of a long corridor, then through another door. They come out in a large room. There are computer screens everywhere and some very flashy machines and laboratory equipment. This is NASTI!

Cat and Ant hide behind a large crate. Peering out across the room they can see several people in white coats. In the centre of the room is a large stone object.

"The statue of Gladstone Day!" whispers Ant.

Standing next to it are Dr X, Plug and Socket.

Move on
Find out if Max and Tiger are there. Turn to page 40.

"Hello, boss!" says Plug.

"We're back!" says Socket.

They walk over to a man in a bright purple suit. It is Dr X.

"At last!" Dr X yells. "Where have you two fools been?"

"Err," says Plug.

"Oh, never mind," says Dr X. "It's time we started to smash up the statue."

"Why are we doing this again, boss?" asks Socket.

"I have already told you once. There are supposed to be some secrets about micro technology inside. Gladstone Day hid them in there when he made the statue."

"Oh," say Plug and Socket together.

"Now, where are the hammers?"

"Hammers?" says Plug.

"Aggghhhh! Do I have to do everything myself?" screams Dr X.

"Look," says Max, from the pocket.

On the other side of the room, he spots Cat and Ant. They have just sneaked into the room and are hiding behind a crate.

"What are they doing here?" asks Tiger. He starts to wave at them, but Max stops him.

"Don't be silly, we don't want to be seen."

"I just hope they know we're here," says Tiger.

"And I *hope* that Ant has a really clever idea to get us out of here!" says Max.

Move on
Find out if Ant has a clever idea. Turn to page 42.

"Where are Max and Tiger?" says Ant.

"My watch shows that they are over there," Cat says. She points to some coats hanging in the corner of the room. "Hang on, I'll zoom in."

She looks through the telescope on her watch and spots Max and Tiger poking out the pocket of one of the coats.

"There!" she says. "Now would be a good time for a really clever idea, Ant."

"I have it," says Ant, after a few minutes. He whispers his idea to Cat.

"It sounds a bit risky. What if you get caught?"

"Have you got any better ideas?"

Cat shakes her head.

"Well then," says Ant. "You'd better shrink then. You need to be on standby with the micro-buggy."

Move on
Turn to page 42.

Just then, Dr X storms out of the room.

Ant seizes his chance. While no one is looking, he crawls along the floor, keeping to the shadows. Micro-Cat follows in the micro-buggy.

Finally, Ant reaches the coat hook. He puts on one of the spare lab coats. It is a bit big, but he rolls up the sleeves. Then he reaches down to where Max and Tiger are hiding in the pocket of Socket's coat.

"Hi," he whispers, picking them up gently.

Max and Tiger are shocked but very pleased to see him.

"What are you doing here?" asks Tiger.

"It's a long story."

"We need to get out of here and take the statue with us. Dr X wants to destroy it," explains Max.

"We can't let him!" says Ant.

"I know," says Max. "In the pocket of that coat is a false beard. Put it on, it will help your disguise."

Ant puts on the beard. Then he puts Max and Tiger on the floor.

Cat pulls up in the micro-buggy.

"Hi, guys!" she says, cheerily.

Move on
Turn to page 44.

As Ant stands up, a large finger prods him in the back.

"Hey you!" says a deep voice. It is Plug. "Get back to work."

Ant gulps. He walks over to a workbench covered with lots of bits of equipment.

"How are we going to get the statue away from here?" Ant asks himself.

Then he spots something on the bench.

"A *Gladstone What-chip*," he says. Ant picks it up and sticks it in his ear. Then he thinks really hard about their problem.

The chip whirs in his ear. Then all of a sudden, he has the answer.

Ant goes over to a keyboard and starts to type. He reprograms the computer. All the screens in the room start to go fuzzy. Then a children's television programme comes on.

Plug and Socket and all the scientists in the room stare at the screens open mouthed. While their backs are turned, Ant rips off the itchy beard and runs over to the statue. He holds on tightly to it. Then he turns the dial on his watch. He pushes the X and ...

Move on
Turn to page 46.

Cat drives over. Max and Tiger jump out of the buggy and help lift the micro-statue into the car. Then Cat speeds off across the room.

Just then, the door swings open and Dr X comes back in the room carrying a big hammer. Cat puts her foot down.

"What are you doing?" Max and Tiger both scream.

"Don't worry," says Cat.

They zoom through the door just before it swings shut. In an instant they are out in the corridor. They head towards a lift.

"I thought you didn't like lifts," says Ant to Cat.

"This is an emergency!"

The doors open and they drive inside.

Behind them, they can hear Dr X scream, "WHERE'S MY STATUE?"

Journey End

Max, Cat, Ant and Tiger leave the NICE building at high speed. They drive back through the city in the micro-buggy, swapping stories on the way.

Back in the park, they put the micro-statue on its plinth. Then they turn the dials of their watches and grow back to normal – along with the statue. Another micro-adventure is over!

Gladstone Day
The man who wrote
The Science of Running

GREENVILLE NEWS

Scientist Statue Returned!

The statue of the famous scientist Gladstone Day is back in Green Bank Park once again. Inspector Textor of the Greenville City Police Department said that it is a complete mystery how it got back there.

Apparently no one saw anybody bring it back. He also said that they will be putting in place extra security and cameras round the statue from now on so that it is watched 24 hours a day.